Peace Stuff: ENOUGH

"Keep your stuff longer, people"

AVIS KALFSBEEK

Companion to
One More Year

Copyright and Licensing

Contents

"Enough is as good as a feast."

Chaucer (circa 1388–1400)

Mary Poppins (1965)

Bonus

Free eBook & Short Stories

The images in the book were taken directly from *One More Year*, book one in the *Pedro the Water Dog Saves the Planet* series.

Click any image to download a free copy of ***One More Year***, or visit: **aviskalfsbeek/book1free**

Already have *One More Year*? Get 3 fun **Prequels** (*Bird-Bully Besties*, *Lucky Mustard*, and *Giro di Baci*) to learn more about the characters before they got busy saving the planet. Get the prequels here: **aviskalfsbeek.com/3free**

CHAPTER 1

A.E. NELSON 1959 FISHING CREEL WICKER BASKET WITH LEATHER STRAP

High above sea level and within a blink of a peace-loving country, a narrow handle of a state contains one of the deepest, most beautiful, glacier-formed lakes in the world. On a warm late spring afternoon, in a modern time when many say the earth will eventually not sustain human life, a strong swimmer pulls a paddleboard on a crystal clear lake, surrounded by steep, craggy mountains. Her curly black-haired dog sits regally at the front of the board. The silence of the lake amplifies the rhythmic sounds of her stroke and breath.

Pedro Says

Pedro here. Tilly asked me to share a few woofs before we begin.
This little book isn't about guilt. It's about noticing what we already
have and loving it more.

Here's how it's going to go:

First, we'll look at **why this matters** from overstuffed closets to the
bigger world out there.

Then, we'll get into **the good stuff**—the 10 Principles of Enough.

After that, you'll get a few **tools to help you keep what matters**.

And finally, we'll **celebrate** with a little play, a love letter, and some
well-earned peace.

So go ahead. Tape the handle. Patch the pants. Share a story about your
old skateboard or the pan that makes everything taste better.

Let's make less waste, more meaning.

Pedro

CHAPTER 2
WHITE 1978 TOYOTA LONGBED PICKUP TRUCK

Tilly paddles along the shore towards the marina. She and Pedro float by   small, two-room log cabin where flower boxes sit under the front windows, and a bicycle rests on the porch alongside a basket filled with herbs waiting to be planted. A bit further down the shoreline, a gargantuan structure of logs towers over the surrounding trees. Tilly counts twenty-eight windows on the front of the three-story log house. It has a wrap-around porch and boat dock with a guest house beside it larger than Tilly's cottage. There are three SUVs, one luxury sedan, four jet skis, two touring motorcycles, and a thirty-eight-foot travel trailer in the driveway.

Why We're Here

ONE MORE YEAR

Welcome to *Peace Stuff: Enough*, a companion book to *One More Year*.

This began on a hike with my teenage daughter more than 15 years ago. We stood on a mountain overlooking the valley when she said, tears in her eyes, "You know, they cut the tops off of mountains and don't put them back."

That moment crystallized a simple truth: Our choices about stuff have a cost, and that cost is worth our attention. This book offers a gentle path to slowing down and reducing your personal impact on the planet, all by focusing on one simple act: keeping one thing, *One More Year*.

The Unstoppable Rise of Stuff

We live in a time of constant acceleration. Over the last century, the total material stock of human society grew more than twentyfold.[1]

Today, according to the U.S. Geological Survey, each person in the U.S. is surrounded by roughly **six times** the material stuff consumed a century ago.[2] This vast increase is fueled by systems like *Buy Now, Pay Later* (BNPL), which are perfected digital tools that strip away the emotional pain of paying from the immediate joy of acquisition. Like the credit card revolution before it, these tools accelerate consumption, making nonessential impulse buys feel instant, harmless, and free of consequence.

PEDRO SAYS, "HUMANS USED TO HAVE SACRED OBJECTS. NOW THEY HAVE SHIPPING NOTIFICATIONS."

The 60-Second Inventory

We don't like thinking about disaster, but when it comes, it shows us what matters most. When you have 60 seconds, what you grab defines your real values.

Here are stories of real people whose homes were lost, or nearly lost, and what they managed to rescue.

Erin, evacuee Palisades: "My husband had about 15 minutes to load up the car ... the only thing I could think of was my one-line-a-day journal, which I had been keeping religiously since my first child was just a day old in 2012."

Laura, evacuee Palisades: "Her son ... asked for his diplomas and signed racing gloves. ... On the way out the door, I managed to take a painting my friend had done of my son surfing.

Marta, evacuee Malibu: The first thing Marta grabbed was a book entitled *What I Wish For You* and a handwritten note, both given to her by her mom before she died. 'It's always been my most important possession and has always been the one thing that I would save in a burning fire, hypothetically speaking, before fires were ever a real threat in my mind.'"

Krystal, evacuee Palisades: "In the end, I left it all behind. A lifetime of over-emphatically placing attachment on all of our history and every little item. I did manage to grab my baby blanket, one Mickey Mouse photo album that I knew had old family photos and a small album of our family pets."

Meredith, evacuee Altadena: "Like many people, I thought I would be back home soon. Thankfully, I was already wearing my wedding ring when we evacuated, and I managed to grab my son's favorite blanket. Along with the photos of our fathers, these are the only sentimental items my family has."[3]

In a crisis, we don't reach for things we bought to *impress*; we reach for things we bought to *connect*. These are objects of memory and love.

Ask yourself: If you had to leave in 60 seconds, what three objects would you carry?

When Your Stuff Becomes Someone Else's War

The cost of this constant consumption goes beyond our mental space and our homes. It is a cost measured in global conflict.

The United Nations estimates that roughly 40 percent of all internal armed conflicts in the last 60 years have been linked to the exploitation of natural resources like oil, minerals, and timber.[4] When we buy, throw away, replace, and resupply on a perpetual loop, we participate in a chain of extraction and conflict.

Our desire for *more, cheaper, easier* creates pressure on land, people, and ecosystems. The pile of "stuff" we have does not float above politics and power. It sits squarely in the middle of them.

Peace Stuff: The Reclaiming of Enough

This is the **Why** of the *Stuff Diet*.

Why "Peace Stuff"? Because peace is the presence of wholeness. It is the necessary state for global flourishing, requiring not only the absence of conflict but the presence of care, conscious equity, and re-centered values in our daily lives. When we choose to keep one thing *One More Year*, we make a choice against scarcity and resource conflict, pouring love into the stuff we have instead of contributing to the demand for what we don't need.

Why "Enough"? Because enough is not just a limit. It is a lens for conscious decision-making, a boundary for peace, and a clear signal that your needs are met.

That's why this book exists. To help you return to what matters, one object at a time. And to remind you...

You are enough.

PEDRO SAYS,
"PEACE STARTS IN THE JUNK DRAWER."

CHAPTER 5
CHOUINARD EQUIPMENT 1972
RED BACKPACK

"So, O M Y stands for *one more year*. I had a dream, about a month ago, about the Crying Indian."

Camas looks confused.

"You know, from the public service announcement in the 70s that tried to get people to stop littering and polluting. We're too young to remember, but the roadsides across the country were a dump full of litter back then," Tilly explains patiently.

"*Indian* is not PC," Camas teases.

"I think the dream was telling me that we need another PSA to curb our overconsumption. That's One More Year."

"Huh?" Camas grunts with her mouth full.

"People should keep their stuff longer. Don't just go get a new cell phone because you're eligible, don't lease a new car because you can afford the payment, don't buy that new outfit because you're depressed and bored."

"I just did all three of those things this month! What's wrong with that?"

10 Principles of Enough

ENOUGH

1. The Power of One

(Inspired by Yvon Chouinard)

2. Say No to Just-in-Case

(Inspired by Eleanor Roosevelt)

3. Replace a Shopping Ritual with a Doing Ritual

(Inspired by Bea Johnson)

4. Store It with Ceremony

(Inspired by George Nakashima)

5. Let It Age

(Inspired by Bill Cunningham)

6. Fix It Like You Mean It

(Inspired by Celia Pym)

7. Ritualize Repair

(Inspired by Tom of Holland)

8. Put a Planet Number On It

(Inspired by Mike Berner-Lee and Kate Raworth)

9. Give It Away (or Buy It for Someone Else)

(Inspired by Robin Wall Kimmerer)

10. The Inner Inventory: You Are Enough

(Inspired by a Chorus of Enough)

1. The Power of One

ONE

"The more you know, the less you need." Yvon
Chouinard

O ne great coat. One honest knife. One trusty bike.

There's something beautiful about a thing that earns its keep year after year, journey after journey.

We don't need fifteen mugs or three can openers. We need one we trust, one we love, one we're proud to lend out and happy to have back.

The power of one is about choosing well, keeping long, and letting time turn use into affection.

Sometimes, one is enough.

PEDRO SAYS,
"I ONLY HAVE ONE KIBBLE BOWL. SCRATCHED. DENTED. MINE."

Example: The Winter Coat

In many households up through the 1940s and '50s, it was customary to own just one good coat. One for warmth. One for walking to school, going to church, and waiting for the bus. A coat that lasted ten years, or was passed down when it no longer fit.

People mended linings, replaced buttons, and turned collars inside out to extend the life. There was pride in a well-worn garment. Practicality and dignity walked side by side.

So how did we end up thinking we needed ten coats instead of one?

Advertising.

By the 1980s, walk-in closets were booming, and fashion seasons multiplied. Rather than something built to last, we were sold many things built to fail or to become "outdated."

The power of one isn't about lack. It's about loyalty.

Architect of Enough: Yvon Chouinard

Founder of Patagonia and self-described "reluctant businessman," Yvon Chouinard spent decades climbing, surfing, and skiing with the same trusted gear, choosing repair over replacement, and durability over trend.

He famously lived out his philosophy of "The more you know, the less you need." Under his leadership, Patagonia launched the Worn Wear program, encouraging customers to repair jackets, re-sew zippers, and keep garments going for as long as possible, and allowing trade-ins of their used clothing. Their website notes, "85% of clothing ends up in landfills or gets incinerated."[5]

A lifelong climber and surfer, Chouinard began forging his own gear in the 1950s because commercial equipment wasn't durable enough.

By the 1970s, his gear-making had evolved into a clothing brand. In 1973, he founded Patagonia, initially focused on outdoor apparel for climbers and later expanding into broader sustainable gear.

Chouinard embedded environmental values into the company from the start, emphasizing repair, durability, and low-impact design.

His ethic was simple:

If it's still working, keep it working.

If it breaks, fix it.

If you love it, make it last.

The company once ran a full-page ad that read, "Don't Buy This Jacket," urging consumers to reconsider before purchasing anything new. That spirit of conservation wasn't just marketing; it was a lifetime of practicing the power of one.

"The more you know, the less you need."

Yvon Chouinard, Let My People Go Surfing

Reflection Prompt

What's something you've kept for years?
What makes it your favorite?

2. Say No to Just-in-Case

TWO

"A little simplification would be the first step toward rational living, I think." Eleanor Roosevelt

"Just in case" is the convenient excuse clutter loves.

It's the backup blender you never use. It's the tangle of mystery cables. It's the coat you might wear if you visit Antarctica one day.

But here's the essential truth: Fear makes us hoard. Peace needs space. And freedom gets boxed up right alongside "maybe one day."

The practice of intentional keeping means we can let some of these objects go.

Wait... I thought this book was about keeping things.

We are! But we are not keeping *everything*.

Quick Test:

1. Have you used it in the past two years?

2. Would you lend it to a friend with confidence?

If the answer to either question is no, set it free. Let someone else love it into usefulness. Your space, and your mind, will breathe easier.

PEDRO SAYS,
"I ONLY KEEP WHAT I SNIFF WEEKLY."

Example: The Minimalists' $20 Rule

Enter The Minimalists, Joshua Fields Millburn and Ryan Nicodemus, modern advocates for intentional living. Through their platforms, they've inspired millions to let go of excess and live with purpose.

One of their mantras is the **$20 Rule**: "If you can replace it in less than twenty minutes for under twenty dollars, let it go."[6]

The simplicity of this rule is the brilliance. So if you find yourself doing the Just-in-Case Cha Cha, use this as a simple guide. Ask yourself: *Is this really worth the space it's renting in my life?*

Here's a quick thought exercise:

Close your eyes.

Picture yourself in your mother's belly. Before you take your first breath, your things pile up. A baby shower. A dozen onesies. Half don't fit by day two of your life. Then come birthdays, holidays, school shopping, souvenirs, hand-me-downs, trends, hobbies, just-in-case cables, second blenders, and free t-shirts.

Now open your eyes.

That mountain of stuff isn't your fault. But it will determine your future if you never question it.

When we keep the right things, the meaningful, the useful, the durable, and release the rest, our lives feel lighter. Our homes breathe easier. And the giant, invisible pile of our lifetime carbon footprint shrinks with every thoughtful choice.

Minimalism isn't about deprivation. It's about devotion to what truly matters.

Architect of Enough: Eleanor Roosevelt

As First Lady, humanitarian, and author of *You Learn by Living: Eleven Keys for a More Fulfilling Life,* Eleanor Roosevelt embraced simplicity not as deprivation, but as clarity.

After losing both parents before the age of ten, she sought purpose beyond material comfort. As First Lady from 1933 to 1945, she redefined the role by holding press conferences, writing a daily column called *My Day*, and tirelessly advocating for civil rights and women's rights. After leaving the White House, President Harry Truman appointed her as a key delegate to the United Nations, where she played a vital role in drafting the Universal Declaration of Human Rights.

She believed that reducing both physical and mental clutter was essential to living with purpose. She traveled light, wore clothes until they wore out, and poured her energy into action rather than accumulation.

For Eleanor, living with less meant living with intention. It freed her to serve more, speak more, and be more.

Reflection Prompt

What's one "just in case" item you could let go of today?
How would it feel to have a little more breathing room?

CHAPTER 13

25' 130 HP 1948 CLASSIC CHRIS-CRAFT SPORTSMAN

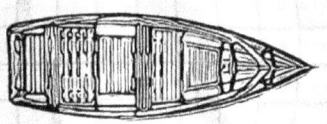

"I've got orders for eleven log homes. Not a single one under 10,000 square feet and the owners want to get underway yesterday. We need these logs now!"

Bear's head sinks and he closes his eyes.

He takes a breath, stands up straight, towering over Gary.

"It's a sad thing. A man spends his entire life sitting in a sterile office dreaming of coming to Montana or Sandglass, and when he finally retires, what does he do? Does he enjoy the land? Does he fish? Does he hike to find wild morels and huckleberries? Does he sit in a quiet kayak with his love? No, he spends the last precious years of his life building a 20,000 square foot ego palace with master suites on opposite ends, chopping down half the forest to do it, when he could have a wonderful life in a two-room cabin."

3. Replace a Shopping Ritual with a Doing Ritual

THREE

"The moment the impulse to buy strikes, I make a dis-ciplined switch: I replace the craving with a 15-minute act of creation." Renee Benes

Sometimes we shop out of habit, boredom, or a hope that something new will fill an emotional hole.

The thrill of a new purchase is fleeting; the satisfaction of mastery and creation is deep and durable.

Instead of scrolling sales or wandering aisles, what if we focused on the infinite abundance of things to do?

The word hobby is defined simply as a regular activity done for pleasure. Online, you can find lists of the top 100, 500, or even 1,000 potential hobbies—from lock-picking to leatherwork, from urban sketching to deep-sea diving. The sheer volume of things you could be doing dwarfs the inventory of any online store.

When you click "Buy Now," your brain gets a steep, temporary spike of dopamine—the "chase chemical." This high quickly crashes, leaving you ready for the next hit.

In contrast, hobbies and physical activities create a different, richer chemical cocktail: endorphins from effort, serotonin from achievement, and oxytocin from sharing a skill. The pleasure isn't in the acquisition; it's in the mastery, creation, and connection that lasts long after the work is done.

These are acts of creation, not consumption. They remind us of our inherent self-sufficiency. Rituals give shape to our lives. Let's choose rituals that remind us we already have enough.

PEDRO SAYS,
"SNIFF OUT A NEW HABIT. LIKE THROWING A BALL FOR THE DOG AT THE PARK."

Example: Renee's Shift from Shopping to Self-Reflection

For years, Renee of The Fun Sized Life blog used shopping as a balm. She'd fill her cart when she was tired, lonely, or insecure, buying new clothes or gadgets to feel better. Over time, she realized those purchases gave back only fleeting satisfaction.

She made a switch: when the purchase itch hits, she now takes a 15-minute pause to sketch, journal, or simply walk away from the screen. That ritual of pausing, reflecting, and drawing gives her space to make a more meaningful choice—a choice often guided by the tools used in recovery: doing versus buying.

In programs like Spenders Anonymous, members replace the emotional high of shopping with meaningful, low-cost rituals: journaling, dancing, walking, or gratitude.[7] The goal isn't just to stop spending. It's to feel whole without it, channeling the energy of impulse into an act of creation or maintenance.

Renee's shift echoes this: choosing presence over purchase. It's a new kind of abundance.

Architect of Enough: Bea Johnson

Author of *Zero Waste Home*, Bea helped launch a global minimalist movement by committing to a life of less. She owns only what she and her family truly need, and replaces shopping with shared projects, outdoor time, and intentional care.

Bea Johnson is a Franco-American environmentalist, speaker, and author, best known as a leading voice in the "zero waste" movement. In 2006, Johnson and her family began intentionally simplifying their lives, and by 2008, she had adopted a zero waste lifestyle.

Johnson formulated a framework known as the 5 R's: *Refuse* what you do not need; *Reduce* what you do need; *Reuse* what you consume; *Recycle* what you cannot refuse, reduce, or reuse; and *Rot* (compost) the rest.

One of her more striking claims is that her family's annual "trash" fits into a small glass jar or pint size. That image helped drive the movement's visibility.

Once a week, she sets aside time to mend, clean, and reassess what her family owns. From sewing buttons to tuning her bike, these acts replace any urge to shop.

"I'm not missing anything," she's said. "I'm just maintaining what I love."[8]

Reflection Prompt

What shopping habit could you gently replace with a doing ritual? What would make it feel special?

4. Store It with Ceremony: Give It a Place of Honor

FOUR

"Have nothing in your house that you do not know to be useful or believe to be beautiful." William Morris

If something's worth keeping, it's worth keeping well, and keeping where you can see it.

Don't bury it in a bin of tangled cords or stash it in the junk drawer of forgetfulness. And don't hide it in the name of tidiness if it deserves to be honored.

Instead, wrap it in cloth. Label it with care. Hang it on a hook. Place it on a shelf that gets morning light. Let your stuff live in dignity, not dust.

Storage is not an afterthought. It's a form of attention. A way of saying, you still matter. It's also a darn good way to reduce the sheer number of things.

Displaying an item is also a kind of respect. It says, "I use this. I love this. This belongs here." When you bring something into the light, be it a quilt, a hat, or a single spoon, you're more likely to use it, care for it, and treasure it.

You don't need more. You just need to show care for what you already have.

PEDRO SAYS,
"I BURY MY BONES IN THE SAME SPOT EVERY TIME. THAT'S HOW I KNOW THEY'RE IMPORTANT."

Example: The Broom in the Alcove

Kawai Kanjiro (1890–1966) was a Japanese potter, writer, and folk craft pioneer who believed beauty lived in humble things. His home in Kyoto, now the Kawai Kanjiro Memorial Museum, shows this belief in quiet ways with spoons laid gently in drawers, brushes arranged with care, and alcoves carved to cradle simple tools.[9]

We don't know if there was a broom in one alcove. But in Kanjiro's world, even a broom would have been honored. It's not hard to imagine one leaning against the wall by the studio door, placed not with haste, but with reverence. A tool, waiting in morning light. A gesture of belonging, repeated each day.

Tiny Home, Big Clarity

In many traditionally small homes (cabins, yurts, boats), there was no "out of sight." Pajamas were folded like a poem. A saucepan rested proudly on its hook.

Today's tiny homes and *van builds* echo that wisdom. You quickly learn what deserves space, and what doesn't. There's no just-in-case storage. No junk drawer. Just one plate. One knife. One perfect sweater for all seasons.

When everything is in view, your mind clears, too. Minimalism isn't punishment. It's a gift, the joy of seeing only what you need, and giving it the honor it deserves.

Across cultures, ceremonial storage has always existed. Furoshiki cloths. Hope chests. Handwritten labels. Tools kept clean and visible. These rituals aren't just about organization. They're about reverence. When you let something rest in a place of belonging, you remind yourself and the world that usefulness is sacred.

Architect of Enough: George Nakashima

George Nakashima (1905–1990) was an American woodworker, architect, and key figure in the American Craft movement. He didn't just design furniture; he practiced an ethical collaboration with nature. His life and work embody the highest form of ceremonial storage and display, honoring the raw, imperfect, and unique quality of a material.

Nakashima's philosophy was rooted in respect for the tree's second life. He purchased large, unique slabs of wood that others deemed "flawed," often featuring knotholes, sap lines, and wild, uneven edges. Instead of concealing these, he emphasized them, stitching and bracing the cracks with subtle butterfly joints. He called this his *Soul of the Tree* series.

He treated the wood not as a resource, but as an irreplaceable, living entity. Every finished table or chair was a conversation between the carpenter and the tree. His pieces were displayed and used with a quiet reverence, meant to last for generations.

His approach teaches us that honoring an object begins with honoring its origin. When we display a table, a bowl, or a tool with care, we are acknowledging the life and resources that went into its making. We give it dignity. We promise to keep its story.

Nakashima wrote, "A small effort is necessary to change the attitude from thinking of a piece of wood as a mere commodity to thinking of it as a gift from the forest."[10]

Reflection Prompt

What's one item you use often but store carelessly?
Where could you place it so it feels seen and loved?

CHAPTER 11
MOTOROLA 1991 STAR-TAC FLIP MOBILE PHONE

"Text? I don't text. I have a flip phone from the 90s."

"How could that possibly still be working?"

"Well, it is still working," he says proudly. "Just like my 1960s boat and my 90s mountain bike. Just like the 1972 microwave that I won't let Suerte stand in front of. Just like my 1978 Honda three-wheeler motorcycle. Just like me!"

"I wish more people were like you. Keeping their stuff longer. It might just save this planet. When you hear from Bear, call me from that flip phone!"

"You got it!"

Tilly gets back onto her paddleboat with Pedro and pushes off the dock.

5. Let It Age

FIVE

"Buy less. Choose well. Make it last." Vivienne West-wood

Softness is not a flaw, patina is not a problem, and wrinkles in coats, frayed seams, and faded hems are simply the fingerprints of memory.

Age adds character. The things we love most are often the ones that show it. Not because they lasted untouched, but because they lasted with us.

Don't rush to replace. Let your things live. Let them tell stories. There's honor in age.

PEDRO SAYS, "SHINY IS SUSPICIOUS."

Some Things That Get Better with Age

- Handwoven textiles that soften over time

- Indigo-dyed cotton that fades beautifully

- Wool felt slippers that mold to your feet

- Quilts passed through generations

- Cast iron skillets (if you use one, keep it seasoned)

- Wood-handled tools worn to fit your grip

- Classic bicycles bearing retro emblems

- Ceramic mugs with nicks in their glaze

- Well-annotated books and dog-eared pages

- Cotton tote bags that remember every errand

- Garden gloves with earth perfume

- Wabi sabi furniture that holds history

- Compost piles (Pedro fact-check: true)

- Friendships, if well-nurtured

- Peaceful routines

- Your favorite trail shoes

(As a sober and vegan human, I chose not to include wine or leather in the patina list.)

Wabi Sabi

The Beauty of Imperfect Things

Wabi sabi is a Japanese aesthetic that honors the imperfect, the impermanent, and the incomplete. For example, a chipped bowl, a weathered book, or a fraying sleeve are not flaws. They are signs of time, care, and presence.

Rooted in Zen Buddhism, wabi sabi invites us to see beauty in age and simplicity.[11]

Ask yourself, "Yes, this is getting old, but is it aging in the right direction?"

Example: The Ship of Theseus

In Greek mythology, there is a famous paradox known as the Ship of Theseus. The ship that Theseus sailed on was preserved by replacing old, rotting planks one by one until every piece of the original wood had been swapped out. The question is: Is it still the same ship?

This thought experiment asks us to honor the *identity* and *story* of an object, even when its material parts change. A coat that has been patched ten times, a tool with a new handle, or a favorite chair with mended springs is still, fundamentally, the same thing. The history of care and repair is what makes it unique.

We are not so different ourselves. Our physical identity is constantly maintained by cellular turnover, where nearly every cell in our body is replaced over the span of a few years. Just as we accept that we remain ourselves despite this ongoing biological renovation, learning to keep and appreciate our things longer may help us accept the beautiful process of our own aging and remaking.

The Ship of Theseus teaches us that longevity is a kind of identity. We keep the memory, not just the material.

Architect of Enough: Bill Cunningham

Bill Cunningham (1929–2016) was the legendary *New York Times* street-style photographer who documented fashion, yet personally lived a life of radical simplicity. For decades, he biked all over New York City, wore the same iconic blue French worker's jacket, and lived in a tiny, book-stacked apartment above Carnegie Hall.

Cunningham's eye was famous for spotting trends, but his personal style was purely utilitarian. He chose the same items repeatedly, embracing their wear and longevity. He believed the garments that lasted were the truest form of expression. He didn't chase newness; he celebrated the story told by repeated use.

The blue jacket, the humble bike, and the simple life were all part of his aesthetic. They weren't just practical; they were a quiet form of protest against the commercialism he documented. He found beauty in the things that were kept, mended, and brought out again and again. His uniform was a way to maintain the freedom to do his work without being corrupted by the industry he covered.

Cunningham said, "Money is the cheapest thing. Freedom is the most expensive."[12]

Reflection Prompt

What's something you own that's aging beautifully?
What makes it more special now than when it was new?

6. Fix It Like You Mean It

SIX

"Keep darning and re-darning, the mended object is going to get good in about 20-30 years!" Celia Pym

When you mend, commit to the process. Stitch slowly and deliberately, perhaps using a bold thread color or a patch from a meaningful source, like a grandfather's shirt or a bandana from a memorable road trip. Mend the object with such pride and care that the repair becomes a visible badge of honor, something you'll want to show off.

Things break—that's inevitable. What truly matters is the choice we make: whether we throw them out or dedicate the effort to bringing them back to life.

PEDRO SAYS, "YOU FIX THE HOLE, YOU KEEP THE SOUL."

Visible Mending

Across history and cultures, from Japanese sashiko to the wartime "Make Do and Mend" campaigns, visible repair has consistently treated damage not as a flaw, but as a feature of lasting beauty.

During the war, fabric was scarce, rationed for parachutes, uniforms, and military gear. Citizens, mostly women, were called on to repair and remake what they had. Leaflets offered advice on turning suits into skirts or socks into mittens. Darning became a patriotic act.

It was less about frugality and more about care: for your home, your country, your future. While we are not in a world war now, we can still do our part for the planet. Every mended seam is a protest against planned obsolescence.

Visible mending is a kind of love letter: to the person who first wore it, to the planet that made it, and to the story it still wants to tell.

Architect of Enough: Celia Pym

Celia Pym approaches repair with reverence. She often speaks of the tenderness in mending, the way holes can reveal not just wear and tear, but the intimate contours of someone's life. Her stitches are visible in bright thread, like applause for everything that item has been through.

Celia Pym, born in 1978 in London, studied visual art and later trained in textiles at the Royal College of Art. Though now known around the world for her work in visible mending, her practice began quietly, evolving through close attention to worn garments and the stories they held.

Pym's work centers on clothes that have been shaped by real lives: a sweater worn during long hospital shifts, a sock rubbed thin by daily walks, a cardigan marked by years of use. These aren't perfect objects. They're lived-in, frayed, and full of memory.[13]

Reflection Prompt

What's the last thing you brought back from the brink?
What did it teach you about care and sufficiency?

7. Ritualize Repair

SEVEN

"I don't think punk ever really dies, because punk rock attitude can never die." Billy Idol

What if once a month, you sat down with your mending basket or toolbox as if it were a date? What if friends joined you?

We live in a throwaway culture, but repair is a quiet rebellion. It's not old-fashioned. It's punk.

What Is Punk, Anyway?

Punk isn't just loud music and spiked hair. It's a do-it-yourself (DIY) mindset that says, we don't need permission to fix what's broken. It's anti-waste. Anti-hype. Anti-pretending-you-don't-care. It's also community—repair nights, bike co-ops, tool shares, helping each other out with whatever we've got.

And did you know that Punk ethos has always included fighting for and standing with the underdog?

Repair is punk. Reuse is punk. Pulling a bicycle out of the neighbor's free pile and fixing it with the volume turned up. Punk.

Example: The Repair Café Movement

In 2009, journalist and activist Martine Postma launched the first Repair Café in Amsterdam. The idea was simple: bring neighbors together with broken toasters, torn jeans, or squeaky bike wheels, and fix them.

Since then, the movement has spread worldwide. Local cafés now operate in Berlin, Toronto, Portland, and beyond, often hosted in libraries, churches, or schools. People do not just repair *things*; they repair community connections.[14]

Architect of Enough: Tom of Holland

Tom van Deijnen, known professionally as Tom of Holland, is a UK-based textile artist and founder of the Visible Mending Programme. He started the community program at his local Brighton Repair Café because he found people wanted to mend their clothes and just needed a little help to get started.

His work features techniques like Swiss darning and transforms worn socks and sweaters into stitched works of art. He encourages others to see repairs not as shameful but as badges of honor, celebrating visible stitches that tell a story.

For Tom, mending is not nostalgia; it is an ethic. Through each visible stitch, he invites us to reclaim meaning and beauty in what lasts.

Tom says, "I like mending to be visible, as it's a talking point which helps me explain to people why I feel it's important to try to extend the life of a garment as long as possible, rather than throwing it out and buying yet another cheap piece of clothing that will disintegrate after a few washes."[15]

Make Repair a Ritual

Create a Mend Me Box. Place a small crate or basket where things go before the trash. A sock with a hole. A chair with a wobble. A hinge that squeaks.

Schedule a Fix Day. Mark it on your calendar: the first Sunday of every month. Alone or with friends. With tea, music, and the scent of something baking.

Build Your Mender's Circle. Shoe repair, tailors, tool libraries, and makerspaces are everywhere once you start looking. Make a list. Support them. Share it with your friends.

Host a Fix Circle. Invite a handful of friends or neighbors. Each brings one thing to fix. Share tools, tips, and snacks. You will leave with more than a mended item; you will leave with community.

PEDRO SAYS,
"SOME SAY THE RISE OF STUFF BEGAN WITH THE DISCOVERY OF THE WHEEL. I SAY IT WAS THE GARAGE."

Reflection Prompt

What is something you threw out that you could have repaired? What would it take to say yes to fixing next time?

8. Put a Planet Number On It

EIGHT

"The most sustainable garment is the one already in your wardrobe." *Orsola de Castro*

We don't see the real price tag. A cotton T-shirt might cost $12 at the store, but producing that shirt can consume more than 700 gallons of water from field to factory.[16] A smartphone can require up to 200 pounds of raw materials, drawn from countries across the globe, to assemble a device that fits in your palm.[17] And that's not even getting to the impact of the waste.

What if we paused to ask: What's the planetary price?

We label our groceries with calories and ingredients, but most of us have no idea how much carbon, water, land, or energy was spent to make what we buy.

I wouldn't say it's easy to figure that out yet, but there are ways to get inspiration and check in on our carbon footprint to keep it top of mind.

PEDRO SAYS,
"THAT T-SHIRT? 700 GALLONS OF WATER. I COULD'VE SWUM LAPS IN IT."

Example: The Planet-Check Jacket

Orsola de Castro, a London-based designer and cofounder of Fashion Revolution, is known for her commitment to making fashion ethical and transparent. After the tragic Rana Plaza garment factory collapse in 2013, she co-launched a global movement demanding accountability across the industry.

In one powerful project, De Castro traced the environmental footprint of a mass-produced denim jacket: 1,000 gallons of water and 30 pounds of CO_2 emissions for a single fast-fashion piece. Instead of buying new, she chose to repair and repurpose an old jacket.

Her decision avoided further emissions, preserved natural resources, and aligned with her call to care for clothes like the good friends they are.

Architects of Enough: Bananas and Donuts

Mike Berners-Lee

Mike Berners-Lee is a British professor and a leading expert in carbon footprinting. He is best known for his practical and deeply researched book, *How Bad Are Bananas? The Carbon Footprint of Everything*.

Berners-Lee's genius is making the planet number tangible. He takes complex supply chains and translates them into understandable carbon costs. What is the environmental price of a text message? A cheeseburger? A single cup of coffee? By providing these precise figures, he forces us to confront the hidden cost of convenience in every choice we make.

His work is a fundamental argument for "Enough." It's not about demanding perfection; it's about providing the data that allows us to make small, informed trade-offs that collectively make a difference. His approach is rooted in the simple insight: you can only manage what you measure.

When we talk about limiting carbon and consumption, we can't forget that there are still millions of people on the planet who need to consume more just to live a decent human life, not an extravagant one. This is where our next Architect of Enough comes in.[18]

Kate Raworth

Kate Raworth is a renegade economist and a senior research associate at the University of Oxford. She is the creator of the *Doughnut Economics* model, which provides a clear, measurable framework for a sustainable and just economy.

Raworth's work answers the question, "What is the planetary price?" by giving us a target zone. This target is the Doughnut, the sweet spot where humanity can thrive. This safe and just space is bounded by two circles: an inner ring, which is the *social foundation* (ensuring everyone has food, housing, and justice), and an outer ring, which is the *ecological ceiling* (staying inside the planet's boundaries for climate, water, and biodiversity). The goal is to move everyone out of the donut hole (the space of human deprivation) and safely into the Doughnut itself.

Her approach fundamentally shifts the goal of economics from infinite growth to achieving balance and sufficiency. If an economic activity pushes us outside the ecological ceiling, it is fundamentally a failure. Her model transforms the abstract concept of "sustainability" into a precise, measurable challenge.

OK, that was the big picture in bananas and donuts. What about our individual purchase decisions? If we can count calories, we can count carbon. These tools help reveal the invisible cost of everyday choices.[19]

Some Planet Footprint Calculators

Carbon Footprint Calculator
ClimateHero
Earth Hero App
Clever Carbon
WWF Footprint Calculator
Water Footprint Calculator

Idea: Create your own "Planet Number" log. Choose one item each week. Look up its carbon footprint by searching,

"What is the carbon footprint of _____?"

Then ask yourself, "What would I choose now?"

Reflection Prompt

Think of one item you've purchased in the last year?
Would you still buy it today? Why or why not?

9. Give It Away

(OR BUY IT FOR SOMEONE ELSE)

NINE

"Reciprocity is a two-way relationship, a dialogue between us and the world. We give our gifts to the land, and in return, the land gives us what we need." Robin Wall Kimmerer

If the restless impulse to acquire still lingers, this principle suggests a powerful counter-action: turn the cash register around and give. This is not about traditional charity. It is a fundamental disruption of the acquisition cycle. By choosing to give, we actively interrupt the constant impulse to accumulate, transforming a feeling of lack into one of abundance and flow.

PEDRO SAYS, "YOU CAN'T KEEP EVERY BALL. TRUST ME, I'VE TRIED."

Example: Burning Man's Radical Gift

At Burning Man, the annual temporary city in the Nevada desert, cash is almost entirely irrelevant. The entire social fabric is built upon the *Gift Economy*, where everything from elaborate meals and performances to a refreshing drink on a hot day is a gift with no expectation of immediate return. This system of radical generosity breaks down market dynamics and fosters communal trust.

However, this generosity is governed by the rule *Leave No Trace.*

Any debris, no matter how small, is called MOOP (Matter Out Of Place). This includes glitter, abandoned furniture, packaging, and forgotten gifts. The MOOP principle is the required counterbalance to the Gift Economy. If you bring something into the world, you are radically responsible for it, from creation to disposal.

We can learn from Burning Man: True generosity carries care, not waste. You can gift freely (art, food, joy), but you must also ensure that nothing you give becomes someone else's burden or the desert's trash. In our case, the planet's trash.

The *gift economy* and *leave no trace* (no MOOP!) melds generosity with stewardship.[20]

Architect of Enough: Robin Wall Kimmerer

Robin Wall Kimmerer, a botanist and member of the Citizen Potawatomi Nation, is a powerful voice for ecological sanity and a rethinking of our economy. In her book, *Braiding Sweetgrass*, she reframes the earth's natural resources not as capital to be exploited, but as gifts requiring reciprocity.

She challenges the fundamental economic premise that land or life can be bought and sold. Instead, she teaches that when we harvest a strawberry, the gift is complete only when we offer gratitude in return, and that gratitude is expressed through stewardship and care for the rest of the strawberry patch. The currency is not money. The currency is respect.

Kimmerer argues that we have been educated to think like consumers, taking what we want without acknowledging the source or the gift. The path to *enough* is to become inhabitants again, practicing the deep reciprocity of a gift economy with the living world.[21]

The Modern Gift Circle

Before consumer holidays took over the calendar, nearly all cultures practiced some form of communal gifting. The goal was never accumulation; it was balance and social cohesion.

That spirit is resurfacing as a direct response to consumerism's pressure on the planet. Some examples are:

- *Buy Nothing Project* groups now connect over 10 million neighbors online, facilitating the free exchange of goods and services without cash.[22]

- Japanese *mottainai markets* honor the ethical and moral act of reuse and avoiding waste.

- In Africa, the Kenyan *harambee* tradition means "all pull together." It manifests as communal fundraising for individual needs like weddings or funerals, or for local projects like building schools and clinics.

- *Makers Markets*, such as NextFab in Philadelphia and Artisans Asylum in Somerville, along with *clothing swaps*, such as Radical Clothes Swap in Los Angeles, prioritize temporary access over permanent ownership.

When the urge to buy strikes, try redirecting that energy. Giving opens life to connection and abundance.

Reflection Prompt

Think of one item you use regularly that you could easily share, lend out, or pass on when you are finished with it.

Instead of a material gift, what is one skill or experience you could offer as a gift to a neighbor this week?

10. Inner Inventory: The Chorus of Enough

TEN

"When your soul is awake, you are a stranger in the world of the clever and the calculating. You are rooted in a place of belonging and you will not be swayed by the transient promises of culture or society." John O'Dono-hue

In nine principles of enough, we have focused on the relationship between you and your things: measuring them, mending them, and moving them along. But this last principle is the quiet culmination of the entire journey. It is the final shift from a consumer's life to a steward's ethic.

The clutter we are clearing isn't just physical; it's the space we used to store the hope that the next thing would fix us.

The ultimate principle of enough is recognizing that your own internal inventory—your self-worth, your skills, your passions, and your dignity—is already complete. You are not a lack that needs filling. You are an abundance that needs direction.

Reclaiming the Energy of Lack

Every dollar spent chasing status or covering an insecurity represents energy that could have been invested in skill, connection, or rest.

When we feel inadequate, we buy a proxy for competence: *I need this expensive notebook to be a serious writer. I need this new tech gadget to start my business.* When we feel lonely, we buy a proxy for connection: *I need to this new outfit to be confident.*

The goal now is to recognize the feeling *before* you shop. Catch the impulse and ask yourself: What is the internal strength I am trying to purchase right now?

This reclaims the immense, precious energy you were spending on external validation, and grounds it back inside your own life.

PEDRO SAYS,
"ONE TAIL WAG IS WORTH MORE THAN TEN TOYS IN A BOX."

Example: Karen Kingston's Quiet

Karen Kingston, a pioneer of space-clearing practices, often told the story of a client who cleared an entire room of "someday stuff." That client slept soundly through the night for the first time in years.

It wasn't the *mere absence* of the physical objects that brought her peace. It was the *deep quiet* that settled into the space after the clutter was gone. The simple act of clearing created a profound energetic shift.

Architects of Enough: A Chorus

Enoughness doesn't come in one style. It isn't always soft or loud, humble or bold. It shows up as quiet resolve and fierce self-trust.

Nora Ephron, writer, playwright

"Above all, be the heroine of your own life, not the victim."

Mahatma Gandhi, peace activist

"I will not let anyone walk through my mind with their dirty feet."

Pattie Gonia, drag queen, singer

"If you feel dead inside, get the f--- outside."

Maya Angelou, poet, memoirist

"I don't trust people who don't love themselves and tell me, 'I love you.' ... There is an African saying which is: Be careful when a naked person offers you a shirt."

Marcus Aurelius, emperor, stoic philosopher

"Nowhere you can go is more peaceful—more free of interruptions—than your own soul."

Frida Kahlo, painter

"Fall in love with yourself, with life, and then with whoever you want".

Ralph Waldo Emerson, author, philosopher

"Nothing can bring you peace but yourself. Nothing can bring you peace but the triumph of principles."

Greta Thunberg, environmentalist, activist

"We can't just choose to tell some facts and not others *because we don't want to upset* people. *We have to tell it like it is."*

Michel de Montaigne, philosopher

"The greatest thing in the world is to know how to belong to oneself."

Alice Walker, novelist, political activist

"The most common way people give up their power is by thinking they don't have any."

Alok Vaid-Monon, performer, poet

"I don't wait for validation from others, I give it to myself, darling!"

Tina Fey, comedian, actress

"Do your thing and don't care if they like it".

Michelle Obama, attorney, former First Lady

"Whether you come from a council estate or a country estate, your success will be determined by your own confidence *and fortitude...Confidence sometimes needs to be called from within. I've repeated the same words to myself many times now, through many climbs: 'Am I good enough? Yes, I am.'"*

Fred Rogers, TV show host, puppeteer

"You don't have to do anything sensational for people to love you."

PEDRO SAYS,
"CHASE YOUR OWN TAIL,
NOT SOMEBODY ELSE'S."

Be yourself, undimmed.

Reflection Prompt

What strength or joy do you already carry that no store could sell you?

What is your personal message of being or having *enough*?

CHAPTER 23

UPCYCLED SUITCASE 2010
THUMPCASE RENEGADE ONE
MOBILE PARTY BLUETOOTH
BOOMBOX

Tilly turns to Graeme, "Here's my why." She takes a deep breath. "I want to send a message for One More Year. I want Liz to make a kit for me that says, *keep your stuff longer, people.* We need to stop all of this crazy overconsumption."

The guys nod their approval.

Tilly continues with a serious look, "I don't want a sponsor. Even if only one person notices and asks what my jersey means, that would mean something."

"Nice," Reeve says.

"Right on," Cutter agrees.

Ike looks proud and gives her a thumbs up, "You go, girl!"

From Principle to Pact

Y ou've just moved through ten *principles of enough* for a quieter, more abundant life. You've met the Architects of Enough and learned the rituals of care. The work of shifting your mindset from consuming to conserving is already in motion.

Before you turn the page and step into the next phase of this guide, pause. Let the dust settle.

Write down one single change you're ready to make, and why that change matters to your future self.

Please put this in your journal:

"What is one change I am ready to make, and why does it matter to me?"

PEDRO SAYS,
"I USED TO BARK AT THE MAILMAN. NOW I JUST JOURNAL ABOUT IT."

The Pocket Play Introduction

A Very Short Play

Adapted from the book *One More Year*

by Avis Kalfsbeek (Approximately 10–12 Minutes)

For some of us, simplicity comes easy. For others, we carry emotional baggage, and also seventeen backup snacks.

You just made (or considered making) your own *Pact* on the previous page. Now, see what happens when Tilly, Camas, and Pedro make their own.

This scene is pulled directly from *One More Year,* the first book in the Pedro the Water Dog Saves the Planet series. It features Tilly, Camas, and Pedro on a hike, on a mission, and on the edge of a vow that could change the world.

If you love this moment, check out the full book for the whole journey. Download the free eBook here: **https://aviskalfsbeek.com/book1free**.

And if you're a minimalist in training, consider this your warm-up hike.

CHAPTER 24

ANTIQUE MELIOR FRENCH
PRESS WITH BAKELITE HANDLE

"Well, if she's any good, you should be able to find a sponsor or two."

"She doesn't want to ride for a sponsor."

"Why is that?"

"She wants to promote a cause instead."

"Well, that would be a first. What cause?"

"I don't know all the details, but it has to do with curbing our overconsumption. She has a clever slogan. One more year. Asking people to keep their stuff longer instead of buying something new."

"Hmmm. Naïve, but interesting."

"There have been some equally naïve ideas that have changed the world."

One More Year: The Hilltop Pact

A 10-Minute Play

This short play, adapted from *One More Year*, features Tilly, Camas, Pedro, and an optional chorus of Overconsumers and Keepers. It runs about 10 minutes on stage and is set on a hillside trail overlooking a lake.

CAST

TILLY

Steady, idealistic, focused

CAMAS

Funny, impulsive, loyal

PEDRO

Dog narrator, in black with necktie of white curls, such as curled white ribbon; speaks directly to the audience

Optional Chorus:

THE OVERCONSUMERS

One or more performers who exaggerate clutter

AND DISTRACTION. THEY CARRY OR WEAR OBVIOUSLY "TOO MUCH"—AN OVERSTUFFED BAG, EXTRA ACCESSORIES, OR ITEMS THAT JINGLE OR GET IN THE WAY. THEIR ENERGY SHOULD FEEL BUSY AND HUMOROUS, NEVER MOCKING.

THE KEEPERS

ONE OR MORE PERFORMERS WHO EMBODY SIMPLICITY AND CARE. EACH HOLDS A SINGLE MEANINGFUL OBJECT AND MOVES WITH CALM, INTENTIONAL FOCUS. THEIR PRESENCE PROVIDES CONTRAST TO THE OVERCONSUMERS.

SET

A HILLSIDE TRAIL. ONE LARGE ROCK. AN IMAGINED LAKE BELOW.

OPTIONAL: A SIDE SPACE FOR THE OVERCONSUMERS (BAGS, BOTTLES, CLUTTER), AND A SIDE SPACE FOR THE KEEPERS (EACH WITH ONE MEANINGFUL OBJECT).

One More Year: The Hilltop Pact (A 10-Minute Play)

(TILLY runs onstage, Pedro zig-zagging with joyful energy. She breathes deep, peaceful. A moment later—CAMAS stumbles in, panting, her backpack absurdly overstuffed. She wears a windbreaker, sunglasses, and slightly panicked joy.)

CAMAS

What the fungus, Tilly, slow down! Stop and smell the pine needles. I thought we were hiking, not chasing your personal best.

TILLY

I do smell them. As I sprint past them.

(CAMAS gives her a look—then melts, flopping down next to the boulder. Her pack hits the ground with a thud. She digs for something—maybe food—but the bag starts coughing up these items below, or similar items, pizza required.)

(Optional Chorus: Overconsumer(s) crowd in, mirroring her clutter. A Keeper(s) stands calm at the far side with one object.)

Items spill out quickly in rhythm; don't belabor each one. Items such as:

A phone charger

A crushed kombucha can

A worn journal

A hoodie

A half-knitted sock

A stress ball

An unopened lip balm

A mason jar labeled "Tea for Emergencies"

A tin of mints

A reusable straw

A second, tinier backpack

A cold slice of pizza

CAMAS

(frantically shoving things back in)

Hold on, hold on. Just need my hydration.

(She pulls out a small, ceramic, decorative cat statue, or similar.)

CAMAS

Ah. Not that. That's for good luck, and a conversation starter, obviously.

(She pulls out a single ice skate, or boot, covered in glitter.)

CAMAS

Oops. Wrong season. And wrong foot.

(She pulls out a jar of pickles and a rubber chicken.)

CAMAS

Right! Trail snacks. And backup emotional support. You never know when you need both a pickle and a good laugh.

(She reaches in deeper, struggling. Her arm disappears up to the elbow.)

CAMAS

(grunting)

Why is there always one more thing at the bottom...?

(She yanks out bicycle handlebars)

CAMAS

Oh....Yeah.

Those.

TILLY

(deadpan)

You brought handlebars?

CAMAS

(shrugs, totally casual)

For... ambiance.

(She tosses them down beside her or sets them leaning against the rock. They stay visible for Pedro later.)

(Camas is surrounded by clutter. TILLY quietly unfolds a small cloth, smooths it on the ground. She places one piece of fruit or bread in the center, ritual-like. A pause.)

(Then—PEDRO freezes, turns toward the audience, and raises a paw toward them.)

PEDRO

(steps toward Camas's pack, to audience)

I'll take those...

(He takes the handlebars. Holding them sideways, he begins "cycling" — legs, shoulders, whole body engaged.)

(PEDRO uses the handlebars throughout his monologue: holding them sideways like a pulpit, "cycling" with full-body pedaling motions to punch up facts, and adding exaggerated swerves when talking about being off-course. At key moments, he may turn the dowel vertically and use it like a microphone for comedic emphasis. Actor may interpret rhythm.)

(Optional Chorus: Overconsumers exaggerate their clutter; Keepers remain steady.)

PEDRO

(to audience)

Pedro Fact Check:

(pedals slowly, like weighing the number)

The average American owns over 300,000 items.

That's like... if every sock and spoon threw a family reunion.

The average hiker brings 293 of them on day trips.

(swerves handlebars toward CAMAS, holding the look until audience laughter lands)

Camas is shooting for the record.

(steady, pulpit grip, weight of fact)

We throw away 81 pounds of clothes every year.

That's a Great Dane... per person.

And none of us even get the dog.

We buy a million plastic bottles every minute.

That's faster than popcorn at the movies.

Only less tasty and way harder to recycle.

Every single day, 13 million phones get tossed. Most of them still work.

And we lease phones with plans to replace them before we even love them.

Imagine dating like that: "Hi, nice to meet you, oh sorry, my upgrade's here."

If stuff were snacks, we'd be buried in granola bars.

If stuff were dogs, we'd be the humans panicking in the shelter lobby.

If stuff were shoes, Camas would have...

(beat, drops handlebars low, conspiratorial)

...actually, never mind. She does have that many shoes.

(beat, gentle)

You can't climb the hill and carry the mall.

PEDRO

But maybe you don't have 300,000 items. Maybe you're doing great.

(He raises a paw, looking genuinely curious)

Let me ask you, has anyone here bought something new recently, maybe a jacket or a gadget, only to realize you already had something just like it tucked away in your closet or drawer?

(Pause for audience reaction, a knowing nod or two.)

It happens. That's why we're watching.

Let's watch.

(PEDRO rests the handlebars back on the crate, careful, like a ritual, then lies down.)

63

CAMAS

(Whispering to TILLY)

When did P start talking?

TILLY

(Shrugs)

(Back to the hilltop. CAMAS has narrowed it down to one bruised apple and the slice of pizza. TILLY has laid out a neat lunch—bread, cheese, fruit—on the cloth.)

CAMAS

What's that OMY on your shirt?

TILLY

(hesitates, then quietly)

It's a project I'm working on.

CAMAS

(takes a bite of pizza, with her mouth full)

I want to hear more.

TILLY

(laughs)

I see you brought one of your five food groups, cold pizza. What are the others again? Ice cream, huckleberries and?

CAMAS

Fries and naps.

TILLY

(shaking her head)

You're one of the strongest people I know despite what you put in your body.

CAMAS

(flexing a bicep)

Food rewards the watts. Why else would we suffer?

(She takes another bite.)

So what's the project?

TILLY

(looks out over the lake)

I see the coal cars passing over the lake on the tracks day after day and I feel so helpless.

CAMAS

What's the big deal? We need that coal to make the cities light up, right?

TILLY

(pulls her beanie down over her eyes to hide her tears, continues slowly)

Did you know that to get that coal they chop the mountain tops off and don't put them back?

CAMAS

(sits close, puts her arm around her)

Oh, you sensitive twit. I love your passion. I prefer passion for handsome guys, but thank goddess the earth has you.

TILLY

(beat—she pulls her beanie up, wipes her eyes, smiles)

OMY stands for One More Year. I had a dream about the Crying Indian.

(Camas looks confused.)

TILLY

You know, from the public service announcement in the 70s that tried to get people to stop littering and polluting. The roadsides were a dump of litter back then.

CAMAS

(teasing)

Indian is not PC.

TILLY

The dream told me we need a new kind of PSA to curb our over-consumption. That's One More Year.

CAMAS

(with her mouth full)

Huh?

TILLY

Keep your stuff longer. Don't just go get a new cell phone because you're eligible. Don't lease a new car because you can afford the payment. Don't buy that new outfit because you're depressed and bored.

CAMAS

(playfully nudges her stuffed backpack)

I did all of those things this month! What's wrong with that?

(TILLY doesn't laugh.)

CAMAS

You know I'm kidding, but I did think about doing those things.

TILLY

It's not just about clutter, Camas. The production of all that stuff generates 45% of all greenhouse gas emissions. If we buy less, the factories don't run as hard.

CAMAS

Wow. That's... a lot.

TILLY

It is. And consider this, the average piece of clothing is only worn seven times before it's thrown out. Seven. Think of the resources that went into that seven wears.

CAMAS

(nods slowly)

Seven wears. That makes my second, tinier backpack feel a little ridiculous.

TILLY

And one more: We're using natural resources 1.7 times faster than the Earth can regenerate them. We're running on an ecological deficit. Keeping what we have is the easiest way to slow that down.

TILLY

I know you can't change overnight.

CAMAS

Okay—wait.

Before I start "letting go," as you like to say...

I need to explain something.

These aren't just *things*.

They're... systems.

Tiny, portable, beautiful systems that keep my life from falling apart on any given Tuesday.

(points to objects as she goes)

This headlamp?

Necessary.

For power outages, night hikes, unexpected spiritual quests—

or when Pedro hides his ball under the deck and we all have to go spelunking to retrieve it.

PEDRO

(soft bark and head tilt)

Fact check: I do that... sometimes.

CAMAS

And this second headlamp?

Backup.

In case the first one fails or I need to lend one to a friend who insists they "don't need gear."

(looks at Tilly)

You know who you are.

This multitool?

It's not a multitool—it's a security blanket disguised as pliers.

These water bottles?

I know there are six.

But each one has a purpose.

Hot days, cold days, electrolyte days, panic days—PMS days--

and one of them still has a sticker from my first bike race.

I'm not getting rid of my race history.

That's emotional archaeology.

And this jacket?

Yes, it's torn.

Yes, the zipper is held together with a safety pin.

Yes, I have four others.

But this one...

This one has been with me through storms.

Literal storms.

And also... stormy storms.

Inside me.

I know it sounds ridiculous, but sometimes these beat-up things remind me I've survived stuff.

They're like little anchors I carry because part of me thinks if I drop them...

maybe I...

Maybe I won't know who I am without all my just-in-case gear.

So no, I'm not ready for a minimalist miracle on this hilltop.

I am a maximalist of memories.

A hoarder of hypotheticals.

A collector of "what ifs."

And honestly?

(raising her voice)

It's comforting.

It makes me feel prepared.

It makes me feel... safe.

(beat)

It makes me feel *me.*

TILLY

Okay — okay — wow.

That was... a lot of feelings for a hilltop.

Can we just take a beat?

Also, I kind of need to pee.

CAMAS

Now?! In the middle of my existential unraveling?!

TILLY

Yes. Now.

This is taking five for friendship.

CAMAS

(grumbling)

Fine. Take your tiny woodland moment.

I'll just... be here... reevaluating my entire identity.

69

(Tilly steps a few feet away, out of direct view but still in earshot. Pedro sits between them like a referee.)

CAMAS

(under her breath, scooping things back into the backpack with dramatic frustration)

I am not a minimalist. I am a survivalist with style.

Each of these things has a purpose — even if the purpose is unclear to you, thank you very much.

This jacket? Emotional armor.

This flashlight? Essential. For... vibes.

This second flashlight? Backup vibes.

This tiny backpack? A backup for my backup vibes.

(continuing to stuff things back in her pack dramatically, examines an item)

This isn't clutter — it's a support system.

A portable ecosystem of preparedness.

I'm not messy.

I'm layered.

Like a lasagna.

A very emotionally complex lasagna.

And yes, maybe I carry too many snacks —

but have I ever let *anyone* get hangry on my watch?

No. No, I have not.

You're welcome, planet.

Look, some people need crystals.

Some people need therapy.

I need... options.

(getting the last few things back into the pack—everything except the

handlebars—she pauses, then sighs)

PEDRO

(soft, sympathetic chuff)

Chuff

CAMAS

Don't you start.

You've got, like, one sock and a stick.

You don't understand my lifestyle.

(Tilly reenters, refreshed, brushing her hands.)

TILLY

Okay. I'm centered.

Are you done whisper-fighting with your backpack?

CAMAS

No.

TILLY

(gentle, but also seeing where this is going)

Okay, okay, calm down, sista.

You don't have to let go of anything today.

(beat — she shifts gears)

How about this:

Is there anything you're *about* to buy?

CAMAS

(thinks... then sheepishly)

I mean... I've been thinking I need a new mountain bike.

TILLY

A new mountain bike?

Really? Yours must be—what—two years old?

CAMAS

(offended in the way only best friends can offend each other)

Judged.

TILLY

(softens instantly)

Okay, okay. No judgment.

But... what if—hear me out—what if instead of a *whole new bike,*

you hit the bike swap and find one really cool used accessory...

and just keep your bike *one more year*?

CAMAS

(grumbling)

One more year, huh?

TILLY

Yeah.

And to commemorate your incredible emotional maturity,

you get your very own "One More Year" T-shirt.

(beat)

Which is technically a new thing...

but it's really just a thrift-store tee with custom iron-ons.

A *symbolic* new thing.

Planet-approved.

PEDRO

(one single bark of agreement, like stamping approval)

CAMAS

......Fine.

That... actually feels doable.

TILLY

(hugs Camas, looks her in the eyes)

If you wait one more year on one of those things, and your neighbor does too, and your mother, and her neighbor, it might slow down the zombie wastefulness.

(louder)

We need to slow all this down!

PEDRO

(two bright barks)

CAMAS

Sold. When do I get my shirt?

TILLY

(smiling)

I'll make you one tonight.

(A stillness. The lake seems to lean in to listen.)

CAMAS

(gentle now)

You're serious about OMY, aren't you?

TILLY

I am.

CAMAS

Then I am too.

(looks around)

Gotta pee too now.

(They rise. Tilly waits as Camas squats behind the large rock.)

CAMAS

(from behind the rock, calling out like she's still mid-argument)

Okay, okay — *what about a new bike in SIX months?*

TILLY

(shakes her head firmly, arms crossed but amused)

Nope.

CAMAS

(still peeing, defeated but dramatic)

Ugh. Fine.

(beat)

CAMAS

(softer, genuine)

Love you, sista.

TILLY

(calls back)

Love you, friend.

(Camas stands up, tries to zip her now-unzippable pack. She gives up, laughing. They walk toward the trail.)

(TILLY runs off.)

CAMAS

(chasing after her, yells good naturedly.)

Slow your skinny butt down!

PEDRO

(paws to pick up the handlebars, to audience, softly)

It starts with a friend's pact.

(Optional Chorus Flourish: The Keepers, still holding their cherished objects, slowly step to form a line across the back of the stage, creating a quiet, intentional final tableau of stability and care.)

TILLY

(from offstage, calls)

P, come!

PEDRO

(barks toward Tilly)

(lifts the handlebars for the vow, holding them vertically, high, like a

beacon)

The hilltop pact is simple:

For one more year, we choose not to replace what still works.

We choose to mend, to share, to appreciate the things we already hold dear.

We choose not the convenience of the moment, but the promise of the future.

One year. One pact. One planet.

That's all we've got.

And that's more than enough.

(Optional Chorus Flourish: The Keepers, still holding their cherished objects, slowly step to form a line across the back of the stage, creating a quiet, intentional final tableau of stability and care.)

(Blackout.)

The Stuff That's Stuffing Us

(FROM THE POCKET PLAY)

PEDRO SAID,

"THE AVERAGE HOUSEHOLD OWNS OVER 300,000 ITEMS."

"...THROWS AWAY 81 POUNDS OF CLOTHING PER PERSON EACH YEAR."

"...BUYS A MILLION PLASTIC BOTTLES A MINUTE."

"...LEASES PHONES WITH PLANS TO REPLACE THEM BEFORE THEY EVEN LOVE THEM."

Hey, was what Pedro and Tilly said in The Hilltop Pact 10-minite play true?

Let's find out...

"The average U.S. household owns over 300,000 items."

TRUE — A *Los Angeles Times* report, quoting a professional organizer, found that the typical American home contains more than

300,000 items. That's a lot of stuff hiding in our closets, drawers, and glove compartments.[23]

"We throw away 81 pounds of clothing per person each year."

TRUE — According to the U.S. EPA, the average American tosses about 81 pounds of textiles annually. That's roughly one giant suitcase... every year.[24]

"...Buy a million plastic bottles a minute."

TRUE (globally) — Worldwide, we purchase 1 million plastic bottles every single minute, according to reporting from *National Geographic*. That's a river of bottles that never stops flowing.[25]

"...Lease phones with plans to replace them before we even love them."

TRUE-ISH — Most phone owners now upgrade every 2–3 years, often because of carrier promotions or lease-style plans. We barely learn our phone's quirks before we send it back into the upgrade carousel.[26]

"If stuff were dogs..." etc.

Pedro metaphor magic — Delightful, but no official statistic compares household clutter to canines (yet).

"Every single day, 13 million phones get tossed."

VERIFIED – This specific figure is cited in the documentary *Buy Now: The Shopping Conspiracy* and reflects the extreme scale of global e-waste.[27]

"The production of all that stuff generates 45% of all greenhouse gas emissions."

TRUE — The UN's International Resource Panel reports that the production and consumption of goods—everything from clothing to cars—creates nearly half of global emissions.[28]

"The average piece of clothing is only worn seven times before it's thrown out."

TRUE — A UK study by Barnardo's found that some fast-fashion items are worn just seven times before being discarded. Seven! That's barely a week of wear.[29]

"We're using natural resources 1.7 times faster than the Earth can regenerate them."

TRUE — The Global Footprint Network calculates that humanity is currently living as though we have 1.7 Earths. (Spoiler: we only have one.)[30]

"The average hiker brings 293 of them on day trips."

More Pedro Math — Not a real statistic. But if you've ever cleaned out your backpack, it might *feel* true.

ONE MORE YEAR PACT

I WILL KEEP OR USE _____

FOR ONE MORE YEAR

INSTEAD OF REPLACING IT OUT OF HABIT, BOREDOM, OR CONVENIENCE.

I'M MAKING THIS PERSONAL PROMISE BECAUSE...

CHECK ALL THAT APPLY)

- [ ] MY BACKPACK IS AUDITIONING FOR HOARDERS: TRAIL EDITION.
- [ ] I DO NOT, IN FACT, NEED SIX WATER BOTTLES WITH DIFFERENT MOODS.
- [ ] I WANT TO KEEP MY BIKE AND MY SANITY ONE MORE YEAR.
- [ ] PEDRO'S FACT CHECKS HIT TOO CLOSE TO HOME.
- [ ] MY CLOSET SIGHED AT ME. LIKE... AUDIBLY.
- [ ] I DISCOVERED DUPLICATES OF THINGS I DON'T EVEN REMEMBER BUYING.
- [ ] I AM NOT A MINIMALIST... BUT EVEN I HAVE LIMITS.
- [ ] THE PLANET COULD USE A BREATHER, AND SO COULD I.
- [ ] I'D LIKE TO SPEND MORE TIME OUTSIDE AND LESS TIME SHOPPING ONLINE.
- [ ] I'M READY TO TRY A TINY REBELLION AGAINST OVERCONSUMPTION.

- [ ] _____

(MY PERSONAL REASON)

MY COMMITMENT:

I PROMISE TO PAUSE BEFORE PURCHASING.

I PROMISE TO HONOR WHAT I ALREADY HAVE.

I PROMISE TO LET THIS ONE SMALL ACT JOIN A LARGER WAVE OF CARE.

SIGNED.

_____

CHAPTER 26
BLACK 2016 CARHARTT SINCE 1889 WOOL BEANIE

Tilly stands up and writes *One More Year* at the top of the paper roll and *keep your stuff longer, people* underneath. Then she adds *Please share what possessions you've had for a long time.*

"Care to get it started?" Tilly asks.

Camas stands up and writes on the paper *Salvo sofa circa 1972, grandma's cast iron frying pan, yard sale 1960's patio furniture. Soul takes time. Triathlete Coach Camas.*

"Thanks, Cam," Tilly says, as she hugs her.

Camas writes, *Tilly headed to Ironman Banff next May* and puts a box around it.

People in the café look over, curious about the wall hanging. A couple stands up and walks over for a closer look.

Necessary Human Possessions

Warning: The following may cause inspiration and mild existential sorting.

N o one will show up at your door to take your ABBA sweatshirt to the thrift store or your *Zenith Wedge* stereo to the minimalist museum.

Your definition of a forever kitchen tool, or a can't-live-without favorite armchair is yours and yours alone.

So proceed with curiosity. Maybe bring a few Post-its labeled "Take to the next chapter," a bit of caution tape marked "Hands off my cast iron pan", and a gentle open heart.

Why Less Matters

We once believed we needed little: a walking stick, a cloak, a bowl. Now, we carry tote bags of tote bags. We endlessly organize, pretending the clutter materialized by itself.

But what if we simply owned less?

This section isn't a prescription. It's a shift in perspective. We are comparing what the world thinks you need to what you truly need.

We've gathered lists from four unexpected companions:

Science for function and survival

Spiritual Sages for meaning and contentment

The Architect's Toolkit for loyalty and action

Materialist Icons for contrast (and a chuckle)

And we've added something more: Your own lifelong list. Your legacy. A life made not of stuff, but of stories.

PEDRO SAYS,
"DOGS DON'T HAVE CATEGORIES OF STUFF. WE JUST HAVE THE HUMANS, THE FOOD BOWL, THE LEASH, THE TRAIL.

Four Views on What We Need

Science Says We Need...

- Clean water

- Weather-appropriate clothing

- A way to cook food

- Shelter from extremes

- Sleep and rest

- Connection with others

- Purpose and learning

Spiritual Sages Say We Need...
- A bowl and spoon (Thich Nhat Hanh)

- One robe or outfit (many monastics)

- A place to sit

- Something to chant or pray with

- A daily rhythm

- A giving hand

- Space for silence

The Architect's Toolkit Says We Need...
- A simple repair kit: needle, thread, duct tape, and a multi-tool for immediate maintenance.

- One digital hub: a reliable phone or laptop to participate in modern communication and commerce.

- Legal identity and means to transact: a wallet, ID, and basic payment methods.

Luxey Aster* Says We Need...
- Silk pajamas (even for camping)

- 4 phones: one for selfies, one for doomscrolling, two for

backup

- A wardrobe mood board consultant

- A custom-designed closet system (preferably climate-controlled)

- Weekly closet edits to keep the algorithm engaged

- An infrared sauna

- ...and at least 7 types of water bottles

* Luxey is a character from Book 6 *Mono Mutante.*

CHAPTER 29
RED AND IVORY 1971 VOLKSWAGEN KOMBI BUS MANUAL 4-SPEED

Camas sits at a table at Heaven's Brothers on her Macbook and scrolls through the One More Year social media page to read recent posts. She is pleasantly surprised by all of the activity. She sees a post with a photo of a washer and dryer that reads *1975 Maytag washer and dryer, Jill Reader*, and another, *1968 Lodge Cast Iron Frying Pan, Chap Walker*.

"You go, Jill. Right on, Chappie," Camas says out loud. She clicks over to an online article entitled, *Sandglass Athlete, Tilly DeMontagne, Heads to Banff Ironman*. The feeling of pride for her best friend and the increasing momentum gives her a boost of extra enthusiasm. She looks up to see Mayor Patrick writing on the kraft paper roll on the wall, *1985 21-foot Wellcraft Scarab 80's boat beetle. Pat O'Connor. Sandglass*.

"That's amazing, Mayor Pat!" Camas blurts out.

He smiles in response. "Well, my wife says I'm cheap, but they don't make things like they used to, and there's no sense in buying new if she's still perfectly good, now is there?"

"Exactly! And stylin'!"

The Forever Possessions List

The Forever Possessions List is intended for you to start your list, not to perfect it, in your journal or in your mind.

Before you begin, cut yourself some slack.

There is no single magic number of possessions. Some committed minimalists aim for a total possession count under 100. Others simply practice Project 333, using only 33 clothing items over a minimum of 3 months. This is your personal blueprint. There is no right answer.

These are the items you already love, or hope to find. They aren't about trend or status. They're about **usefulness, repairability, beauty, and meaning.**

Journal Prompt

Using the categories below as inspiration, write down what you already have that you'd fight to keep:

1. What's missing from your essentials?

2. What could you let go of, with gratitude?

3. If you've been planning a new purchase, could you wait longer to buy it? If you really need it now, can you find it pre-owned? If you buy it new, how will you ensure it lasts as

long as possible?

Lifetime Essentials

These categories are just a spark. Make them your own, and make sure to emphasize durability and repairabily.

Clothing

- A coat
- Three jackets
- Five bottoms
- Five tops
- Five shoes
- Something you'd be proud to be buried in
- (*Optional: Three pairs of socks that spark joy*)

Vogue calls it a capsule wardrobe. Annmarie O'Connor, author of The Happy Closet, calls it a You-niform. Pedro calls it traveling light for the long haul. Keep it simple. Keep it durable. If you add something, make it worthy of the journey.

PEDRO SAYS,
"MY CLOSET IS MY FUR COAT.
ZERO DECISIONS, MAXIMUM DURABILITY."

Kitchen

- One great knife

- One great pan

- A mixing bowl

- One mug that fits your hand just right

- Basic utensils

- Dishcloths that last

- Pedro says: "Don't forget the dog bowl!"

Tools

- Hammer or multitool

- Screwdriver set

- Duct tape

- Needle and thread

- Rechargeable flashlight

- Rechargeable batteries

- First aid kit

(This is a Peace Stuff world, so firearms are not required.)

Travel & Mobility

- A good backpack or weekender bag

- Bike or mobility aid

- Durable water bottle

- Sunglasses

- External battery or solar charger

Comfort

- One soft throw blanket

- A great pillow

- A book light

- Something that smells like home

Work & Creativity

- A pen you love

- A journal or notes system

- Art supplies

- Headphones or earplugs

- Music (purchase directly from the artist whenever possible)

The Forever Log

We all have impulses to buy. That's not the problem.

The Forever Log is here to help you pause—before the click, before the checkout—and ask what you really need.

Try this:

Before you buy something that's not food, shelter, or truly necessary, wait just one more day. Or one more month.

(*One documentary calls this the best anti-consumption habit ever. Sounds familiar, right? One More Year?*)

Then ask:

    1.   What's the real feeling I want right now?

    2.   Is there another way to meet that need?

That's it. No guilt. No rules.

Just a pause. A breath.

And maybe, a new way to tell what really matters.

Try out the Forever Log and see if it slows your consumption. And if you *do* buy the thing? Great. Just log it with care and curiosity, and see if you can keep it longer.

FOREVER LOG

Item	Aquired	Replaced?	Why I Kept (or Want) It	Have / Want
Cast iron skillet	2012	N	My mom's	Have
Record player	——	——	Waiting to find one I'll truly love.	Want
Wool (camel) Coat	2009	N	"Wear it forever" coat. Re-lined twice.	Have
Bike tool set	2020	N	Compact, feels like freedom.	Have

Pedro says:

One paw in front of the other. That's how I quit chewing flip-flops. (Also... this log helps.)

PEDRO'S LOG

Item	Aquired	Replaced?	Why I Kept (or Want) It	Have / Want
Gator Toy	2021	N	Tilly fixed it 3 times. Still squeaks.	Have
Life vest	2020	N	Worn on every lake day. Smells like summer.	Have
Comfy bed (organic)	2023	N	My official napping station. Zero regrets.	Have
Tennis ball (yellow)	2019	N	I lost the first one. This is the superior backup.	Have

CHAPTER 37

VINTAGE EMBROIDERED BUCKSKIN FRINGED HIPPIE WOODSTOCK JACKET WITH CUPPED METAL BUTTONS

"I think the thing I love most about this place, besides feeling the ancestors with me, is peace rock," Tilly says, gazing over to a large smooth oval stone sitting at the top of a nearby mound. "It gives me hope when hope is hard to see."

Frida speaks lovingly "That stone was used by the hundreds of years ago to pound corn and seeds. It is said they realized the prayers they chanted while working were coming true. Every day they moved it infinitesimally small distances towards the top of the sacred mound where all, but primarily men, would go to meet the ancestors in ceremony and prayer. By the time it reached the top, it had taken more than a year, the woman had stopped using it for food by then and instead used it to make offerings of beautiful sacred objects... a feather, a baby's first lost tooth, a stone, a shed antler, a flower. Dear one, when do you find hope so distant?"

"I see so many useless belongings and that creating them is killing the earth."

"We show by what we worship what we are."

Sacred Earth. Sacred Traditions. Sacred You.

(Is Shopping a Religion?)

"Which is more valuable, possessions or your person?"
Tao Te Ching

For thousands of years, teachers and wise people across every culture have told us that our ultimate peace is found within, not without. Our true self is not defined by our possessions. The core message echoes with crystal clarity: Beware of greed and attachment. The wisdom shared here touches on universal themes of detachment, though this list cannot be exhaustive of every global spiritual tradition.

In the religion of shopping, the rituals are practiced daily. The altar is the checkout counter, and the tithe is paid in four easy installments. High priests are called influencers. The holy relics are handbags, smart watches, and ever-changing seasonal decor. In this faith, we are told salvation lies not within, but in the cart. More is holy. Same-day delivery is divine. And the only original sin is being seen in last season's jacket.

Buddhism teaches in the Dhammapada: "Attachment is the root of suffering." Similarly, in Jainism, the principle of aparigraha means "non-possessiveness" or "non-attachment" to belongings.

In **Islam**, a hadith of the Prophet Muhammad reminds us: "If the son of Adam had two valleys full of wealth, he would desire a third. Nothing will fill his belly but the dust of the grave."

The **Bible** says, "Watch out and be on guard against every form of greed, for one's life does not consist in the abundance of possessions."

In **Hindu** philosophy (specifically the Yoga Sutras), aparigraha is held as one of the ethical yamas: take only what is needed, keep only what serves the moment.

PEDRO SAYS,
"I BOW TO THE ENOUGH IN YOU."

Indigenous teachings, particularly those of the Pacific Northwest and Plains nations, emphasize that humans are not owners of the Earth, but stewards. This perspective is often expressed in the sentiment attributed to Chief Seattle: "The Earth does not belong to us; we belong to the Earth." The call is always to live in balance and act with respect toward all living beings.

Judaism emphasizes Bal Tashchit, the ethical prohibition against waste, teaching that destruction and reckless consumption of resources are forbidden. This principle of conservation requires us to use resources with wisdom and respect.

Sikhism teaches that detachment from material possessions (vairag) is a mark of true wealth, honoring simplicity, generosity, and service to others.

The Cult of Consumerism

Buy Now: The Conspiracy of Shopping, a sharp and compelling documentary about the hidden forces behind consumerism. Highlights:

> *"It's a science to get you to buy stuff... The point was to **reduce your time to think critically** about a purchase."* Maren, former Amazon UX Designer

100 Billion pieces of garment are produced globally every single year.

Unsold, perfectly usable merchandise is often **deliberately destroyed (slashed or ruined)** to prevent it from being discounted, thereby protecting brand image.

13 Million phones are thrown out every single day.

Planned Obsolescence dictates that products are designed to break or fail (like batteries) to force replacement.

This long, global tradition of inner order and temperance—whether called *aparigraha* or *Asha*—is not an ancient inconvenience. It is the most modern answer to our global crisis. Our daily choice to slow down, repair, and keep one thing *One More Year* is a sacred act of turning away from the chaos of excess and aligning with centuries of wisdom.

We stand with our sacred possessions: those essential to life, beauty, and love. And in doing so, we commit to building a legacy of peace, not pollution.

CHAPTER 36

NEON-COLORED THRIFT SHOP KIDS' SHOCK PROOF 8X21 BINOCULARS WITH BIRD WATCHING CARRYING CASE

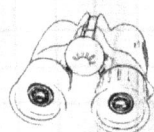

Tilly overtakes rider number four as the athletes near the end of the cycling course. They fall back into position, and she makes her move to advance again and pass the rider in third place. The crowd cheers as Tilly and the other cyclists cross the cycling finish line.

Camas starts a chant with her booming voice, "Tilly! Tilly! Tilly!"

The crowd joins in too. A man in the crowd points to Tilly, "What's OMY?"

Another man with long, blond dreadlocks and rainbow, tie-dyed, baggy drawstring pants and T-shirt, looking through neon-colored kids' binoculars, responds in very slow, stoner speech, "I don't know, man. It's not OMG."

"It's OMY, one more year! She's in third place, and she's never even cycled in a race before!" Camas shouts.

"Holy shit, man. One more year? One more year... one more year," hippie-man chants carefully and slowly.

Best Friend Activism

BE THE EXAMPLE

We just looked at the sacred teachings, the timeless reminders from across cultures that our peace doesn't come from possessions. But knowing a truth and living it are two different things. It's one thing to read the Tao Te Ching and feel serene... and another thing entirely to face a cluttered closet on a Tuesday afternoon.

That's where humor, humility, and a little friendly rebellion come in. You don't have to be a monk—you just need to be a Best Friend Activist.

Remember when Tilly told Camas to keep her stuff longer—just for one more year? She didn't give a lecture. She didn't judge. She packed a picnic and said it from the heart.

That's *best friend activism*.

It's not about yelling on street corners (though some days, that's great too). It's about walking the walk, then gently waving others over to your trail.

Best Friend Activist Moves

Wear visibly repaired clothing and say, "Thanks, I fixed it myself."

Give your favorite book (or kitchen tool) as a gift, with a handwritten note.

Host a swap night, not a shopping spree.

Talk about how much you love your one backpack, not how bad other brands are.

Say, "No thanks, I'm on a Buy Nothing kick," when offered trendy impulse stuff.

Recommend secondhand shops like they're secret treasure caves.

Post about your grandma's rolling pin or your patched-up raincoat.

Let kids in your life see you fixing, cleaning, and cherishing things.

Give your "stuff stories" freely: how you got that jacket, or why you still use that pan.

Let Pedro be your mascot of good-natured rebellion (see below)

Are you an influencer for the planet?

A message from Pedro, who is a very good dog and a very tired one, too.

Look, we need to talk.
We're drowning in haul videos.

Our feeds are stuffed like discount bins with "must-haves" and "it-girls" and "curated links."

You're linking to the same twelve beige water bottles, three linen brands, and one ethically problematic toothbrush.

No judgment. We've all clicked. But here's the thing:

Every product you promote whispers to someone: You are not enough without this.

Let's flip that. Let's start whispering: You are enough. Let's show what it looks like to keep something, love something, repair something. Let's tell the story of your one great coat, your second hand bicycle, your no-filter life.

If you have a platform, use it for something real.

If you don't, even better. Real influence starts in kitchens and classrooms, not in captions.

What the heck is a haul video?

It's a social media video where someone shows off everything they just bought—usually in big quantities and fast fashion.

"Here's my $500 Shein haul!"

"These are all the sweaters I bought this week!"

"Insert store name - haul time—let's unbox it together!"

It's like a shopping brag... filmed.

But here's the catch: Haul culture normalizes overconsumption.

It teaches us to value *new* over *enough*.

What if we made a "Hold" video instead?

Pedro's "Hold" Video

"Hi, I'm Pedro the Water Dog. Welcome to my Hold video. Roxy called. She wanted to go to the Walmart pet section. I told her, Rox, I'm good with my stuff...

I've got one sock. Still smells like my person. Keeping it forever.

I've got a turtle chew toy from 2020. Missing an eye. Still full of wisdom.

I've got a stick from the Great Backyard Storm of '22. Not just any stick. The stick.

That's it. That's the haul!

Peace out."

Low-Key Post Ideas

Optional templates for Instagram, TikTok, or wherever you hang out:
"Kept this for 12 years. Still love it. Still works. Still me."
"Repair date with myself. My jacket and I are back together."
"Not new. Just treasured."
"This was my grandpa's. He called it his lucky golf tee."
"Buy Nothing. Mend Everything. Hug Pedro."

Pedro's Hashtag Menu

Feel free to use these or invent your own:
#BestFriendActivist #KeepItOneMoreYear #RepairedNotRe-placed #LoveYourOldStuff #FixItForward #NoMoreHauls #MenditLikeYouMeanIt #PlanetOverProduct #PeaceStuffEnough

Whistle Blower or Peace Warrior?

Sometimes a hashtag just won't do.

Standing up for a cause isn't always about joining a march or sharing a post. Sometimes, it involves courage, strategy, and organizing with others who share your commitment.

A perfect example of this is the story of Maren Costa, a principal user experience designer at Amazon. Her role was focused on making the online shopping experience easier and faster—essentially, optimizing hyper-consumption. Over time, Costa realized that the core function of her work, accelerating the process of buying more things, was directly contributing to the climate crisis. This realization fueled a powerful movement she joined with her colleagues in 2018.

This group formed Amazon Employees for Climate Justice (AECJ). Instead of just protesting outside, they organized thousands of their colleagues to demand that Amazon create a robust climate plan. They didn't just ask nicely. They used their power as employees to hold the company accountable, proving that a single voice, when joined by hundreds of others, can become impossible to ignore.

Their efforts ultimately led Amazon's leadership to commit to the Climate Pledge, a promise to become net-zero carbon across its business by 2040.

Sadly, Costa and others were later fired for their persistent activism, but their actions demonstrate that being a Peace Warrior sometimes requires being a Whistle Blower, joining a long list of brave individuals who have risked everything to speak the truth, like:

Karen Silkwood, who exposed safety violations at a nuclear facility.

Dr. Jeffrey Wigand, who exposed harmful practices in the tobacco industry.

Sherron Watkins, who alerted executives to massive accounting fraud at Enron.

Whether we're called to be the Batman or the Robin, the headliner or the roadie, there's always a role to play in the show of change.

CHAPTER 40

VINTAGE HAWKEYE
BURLINGTON GREEN AND TAN
WOVEN PICNIC BASKET WITH
PIE SHELF

"If not, OMY is..." Reeve turns towards the other guys. In unison, they all called out, "One more year! Keep your stuff longer, people!"

There is a deafening round of applause. A band plays low folk acoustic guitar behind the guys as one by one they join Reeve at the microphone. Ike comes to the mic first.

"I'm Ike..."

The crowd cheers.

"...and I've had this guitar for thirty-two years. I hope I get to play with the band tonight. When it needed work, Dan in town, who also makes violins for a living, repaired it."

Dan waves from the cheering crowd.

Cutter steps up to the mic, "Howdy. I've kept my cell phone so far for five years. Larry, at the computer shop in town, has fixed my broken screen three times."

Cheering continues.

Josh steps up to the mic, "I've kept these jeans for six years. My mom keeps 'em decent."

Author's Note

THE TALISMAN

T hank you for traveling this journey into *Peace Stuff: Enough*.

The Universe does not judge you based on your inventory. If you only remember one thing from this little book, let it be this: You are 100 percent enough.

A memorial sign near Mahatma Gandhi's ashes displays a quote known as Gandhi's Talisman:

"I will give you a talisman. Whenever you are in doubt, or when the self becomes too much with you, apply the following test. Recall the face of the poorest and the weakest man whom you may have seen, and ask yourself, if the step you contemplate is going to be of any use to him."

We are enough.

Peace and love,

Other books by Avis Kalfsbeek

PEACE STUFF LIBRARY

Pedro the Water Dog Saves the Planet Primers

One More Year (Primer 1)

Plastic Plankton (Primer 2)

Bike Rock (Primer 3)

Copper Cobra (Primer 4)

Planeteering (Primer 5)

Mono Mutante (Primer 6)

Listen & Reflect

Peace is Here Podcast with Avis Kalfsbeek

Join the Community

www.AvisKalfsbeek.com

Free eBook & Short Stories

FOR YOU OR A FRIEND

Download a copy of *One More Year*

Book 1 of the Pedro the Water Dog Saves the Planet series:

aviskalfsbeek/book1free

Already have *One More Year*? Get 3 fun **Prequels** (*Bird-Bully Besties*,

Lucky Mustard, and *Giro di Baci*) to learn more about the characters

before they got busy saving the planet.

aviskalfsbeek.com/3free

Love Letter to a Well-Worn Thing

A Small Meditation on Loyalty

E very once in a while, something stays. It has been with you through moves, messes, moods, and milestones. It's probably not fancy. It might be scratched, soft, faded, or stained. That's exactly why you love it. This page is for that loyal thing.

A backpack. A hoodie. A garden trowel. A chipped mug. A rolling pin. A dog-eared book. Not because it's perfect, because it's yours.

The act of appreciation is not only for the items you release. It is a vow of commitment to the loyal things that remain.

You might be thinking, "What's the point? It's just an inanimate object." But just try it. This simple act of connection can surface lovely or bittersweet memories. It may also cause you to look at your other things with a deeper sense of care, even your humans.

Consider taking a moment and write it a letter in your journal.

LOVE LETTER

DATE: _____

DEAR _____,

YOU'VE BEEN THERE THROUGH

_____

_____

YOU SHOWED UP WHEN

_____

I ALMOST LET YOU GO WHEN

_____

BUT I'M GLAD I DIDN'T, OR IF II DID, I STILL THINK OF YOU.

YOU REMIND ME OF

_____

_____

LOVE,

_____

May you carry on with peace and enough.

The End.

Endnotes

1. International Resource Panel. Global Material Flows Database. UNEP.

2. Wagner, D. T., "The Growth in Material Stocks in the United States, 1900–2018." *U.S. Geological Survey Open-File Report 2021–1018.*

3. Eloise, Marianne. "LA Fires: 7 People Who Lost Their Homes Share the Objects They Saved." *Architectural Digest*, January 31, 2025.

4. UNEP (2009). From Conflict to Peacebuilding: The Role of Natural Resources and the Environment. UNEP.

5. www.Patagonia.com "Worn Wear." Accessed November 2025.

6. The Minimalists (Joshua Fields Millburn & Ryan Nicodemus). www.theminimalists .com.

7. Spenders Anonymous. "The 12 Steps of Spenders Anonymous." spenders.org/abou t.html.

8. Béa Johnson. *Zero Waste Home: The Ultimate Guide to Simplifying Your Life by Reducing Your Waste.* Scribner, 2013.

9. The Kawai Kanjiro Memorial Museum, Kyoto, Japan. Information about the potter's life, work, and aesthetic principles is available through the museum's published materials.

10. George Nakashima, quoted in "The Woodworker as a Humanist: George Nakashima." *Craft Horizons*, Vol. 42, No. 3 (June 1982).

11. Leonard Koren, *Wabi-Sabi for Artists, Designers, Poets & Philosophers* (Berkeley: Stone Bridge Press, 1994).

12. Bill Cunningham, quoted in *Bill Cunningham New York*, directed by Richard Press (Zeitgeist Films, 2010).

13. Sarah Thompson, "The Mender's Tale: An Interview with Celia Pym," Crafts Magazine, no. 280 (Autumn 2020): 45–51.

14. Repair Café International Foundation, "History of the Repair Café," accessed November 25, 2025, www.repaircafe.org.

15. Tom van Deijnen. "A Chat with Tom of Holland." *Kate Davies Designs,* April 20, 2014. https://katedaviesdesigns.com/2014/04/20/a-chat-with-tom-of-holland/.

16. Elizabeth L. Cline, *The Conscious Closet: The Revolutionary Guide to Looking Good While Doing Good* (New York: Plume, 2019), 67.

17. Jane O'Donnell, "The Environmental Cost of Your Smartphone," *BBC Future*, October 3, 2018.

18. Mike Berners-Lee, *How Bad Are Bananas? The Carbon Footprint of Everything* (Vancouver: Greystone Books, 2020), Introduction.

19. Kate Raworth, *Doughnut Economics: Seven Ways to Think Like a 21st-Century Economist* (White River Junction, VT: Chelsea Green Publishing, 2017), 4–10.

20. Burning Man Project, "The 10 Principles of Burning Man," accessed November 25, 2025, https://burningman.org/culture/philosophical-center/10-principles/.

21. Robin Wall Kimmerer, *Braiding Sweetgrass: Indigenous Wisdom, Scientific Knowledge and the Teachings of Plants* (Minneapolis: Milkweed Editions, 2013), 28, 30–35.

22. Alina Selyukh. "The Rise of the Buy Nothing Project and the Gift Economy." *NPR: All Things Considered,* December 12, 2021.

23. Los Angeles Times. "For many people, 'stuff' is a burden that brings them down." May 18, 2014.

24. U.S. Environmental Protection Agency. "Facts and Figures about Materials, Waste and Recycling: Textiles." Last modified March 2024.

25. Laura Parker. "A Million   Plastic Bottles a Minute: Behind the Booming Business of Bottled Water."   National Geographic. June 28, 2019.

26. Consumer Technology Association, "U.S. Consumer Technology Sales and Forecasts," Annual Report, 2023.

27. Buy Now: The Shopping Conspiracy. Directed by Patrick Creadon. 2023.

28. United Nations International Resource Panel. Global Resources Outlook 2019.

29. Barnardo's. "Wears Before Disposal." UK clothing longevity report, 2015.

30. Global Footprint Network. "Earth Overshoot Day." 2023.